PIANO • VOCAL • GUITAR

BILLY
Balla

CONTENTS

C0000 50007 1297

ISBN 0-7935-2326-6

H.L.® Hal Leonard Publishing Corporation

7777 West Bluemound Road P.O. Box 13819 Milwaukee, WI 53213

18555
9.95

AND SO IT GOES

Words and Music by
BILLY JOEL

Slow Ballad, with much rubato

too. And you can have this heart to break.

And so it goes, and so it goes,

and you're the on - ly one who knows.

CAPTAIN JACK

Words and Music by
BILLY JOEL

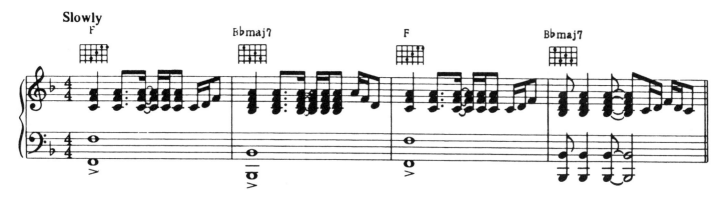

1. Sat-ur-day night_ 'nd you're still_____ hang-in' a - round,_
2. Your sis - ter's_ gone out,_____ she's on a date_
3. So you de - cide_ to take_____ a hol - i - day,_
4. So you play your_ al - bums and_____ you smoke your pot,_

You're tired of liv - in' in your_____ one horse town._
And you just sit at home and_____ mas - tur - bate._
You got your tape deck and your brand new Chev - ro - let.
And you meet your girl friend in the park - ing lot._

You'd like to find __ a lit-tle hole in the ground __ for a
The phone is gon-na ring soon, but you just can't wait ___ for that
Ah but there's no __ place to go an-y way ____ and what
Oh, but still you're ach - ing for the things you have - n't got, what went

while mmm _____
call mmm _____
for mmm _____
wrong mmm _____

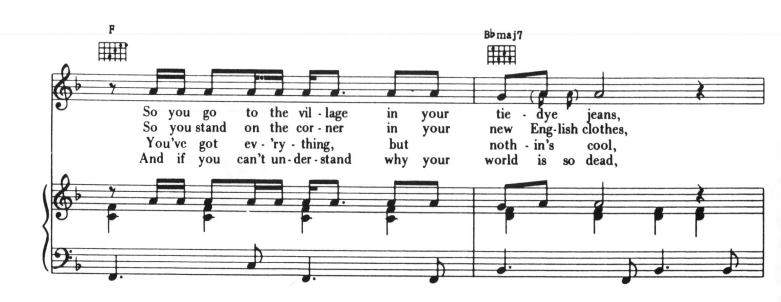

So you go to the vil-lage in your tie - dye jeans,
So you stand on the cor-ner in your new Eng-lish clothes,
You've got ev-'ry-thing, but noth - in's cool,
And if you can't un-der-stand why your world is so dead,

And you stare at the junk - ies and the clo - set queens,__
And you look so__ pol - ished from your hair down__ to your toes,__
They've just found your__ fa - ther in the swim-ming pool,__
And why you've got to keep in style and feed your head,__

It's like some por - no - graph - ic mag - a - zine,__ and you
But still your fin - gers gon - na pick your nose__ af - ter
And you guess you won't be go - ing back to school__ an - y -
Well, you're twen-ty one and still your moth - er makes your bed __ and that's too

smile mmm_____
all mmm_____
more mmm_____
long mmm_____

BABY GRAND

Words and Music by
BILLY JOEL

keep __ those mem-o-ries hold-ing on. __

I've come far

from the life I strayed in;

I've got scars

from those dives I played in.

Now I'm home,

and I'm wea-ry __

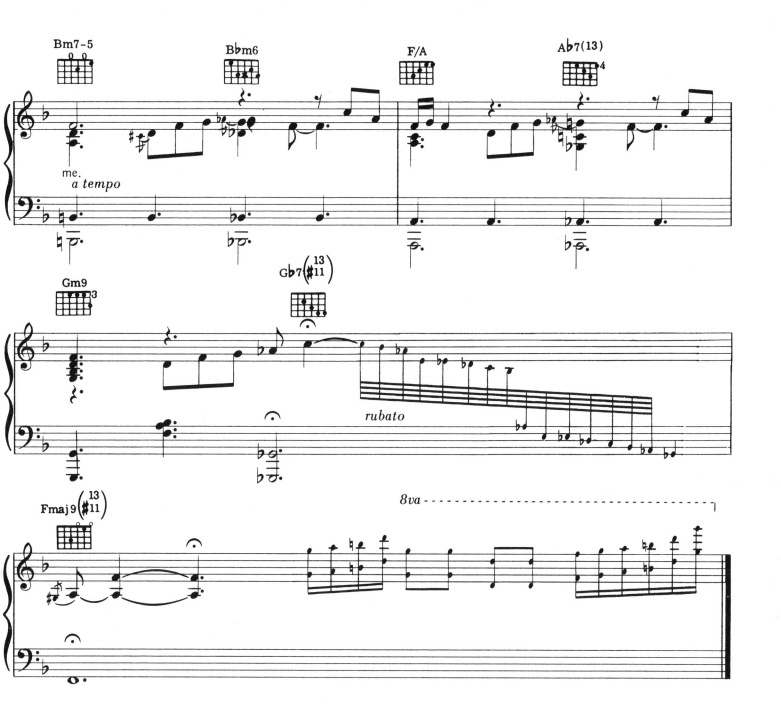

Verse 2:
In my time, I've wandered everywhere
Around this world; she would always be there,
Any day, any hour;
All it takes is the power in my hands.
This baby grand's been good to me.

Verse 3:
I've had friends, but they slipped away.
I've had fame, but it doesn't stay.
I've made fortunes, spent them fast enough.
As for women, they don't last with just one man;
But Baby Grand will stand by me.

(To Bridge:)

52ND STREET

Words and Music by
BILLY JOEL

We're gon-na slip it to 'em short and sweet___ on

Fif - ty___ Sec - ond Street

THE DOWNEASTER "ALEXA"

Words and Music by
BILLY JOEL

Am
C
G
F
- a, and if you work with the rod _ and _ the reel, ___ tell my
C
Dm
C
G
F
wife I ___ am troll -ing _ At - lan - tis, and I still have _ my hands on the wheel. _
Am
G
Am
G
Am
Em

GOODNIGHT SAIGON

Words and Music by
BILLY JOEL

HONESTY

Words and Music by
BILLY JOEL

JUST THE WAY YOU ARE

Words and Music by
BILLY JOEL

LEAVE A TENDER MOMENT ALONE

Words and Music by
BILLY JOEL

In an easy 4 (♩♪ = ♩ ³ ♪)(♩ = about 100)

love ____
Inst. ____

Some - times   I   get   so   a - fraid
just   when   I   ought   to   re - lax

But

E - ven   though   I'm   in   love.

E♭maj7   Dm7   Cm7   Cm7/F

SHE'S ALWAYS A WOMAN

Words and Music by
BILLY JOEL

52

54

D. S. al Coda

Coda

most she will do is throw sha-dows at you But she's al-ways a wom-an to

me. _____ (Hum) _____ (Hum) _____

rit.

THE LONGEST TIME

Words and Music by
BILLY JOEL

58

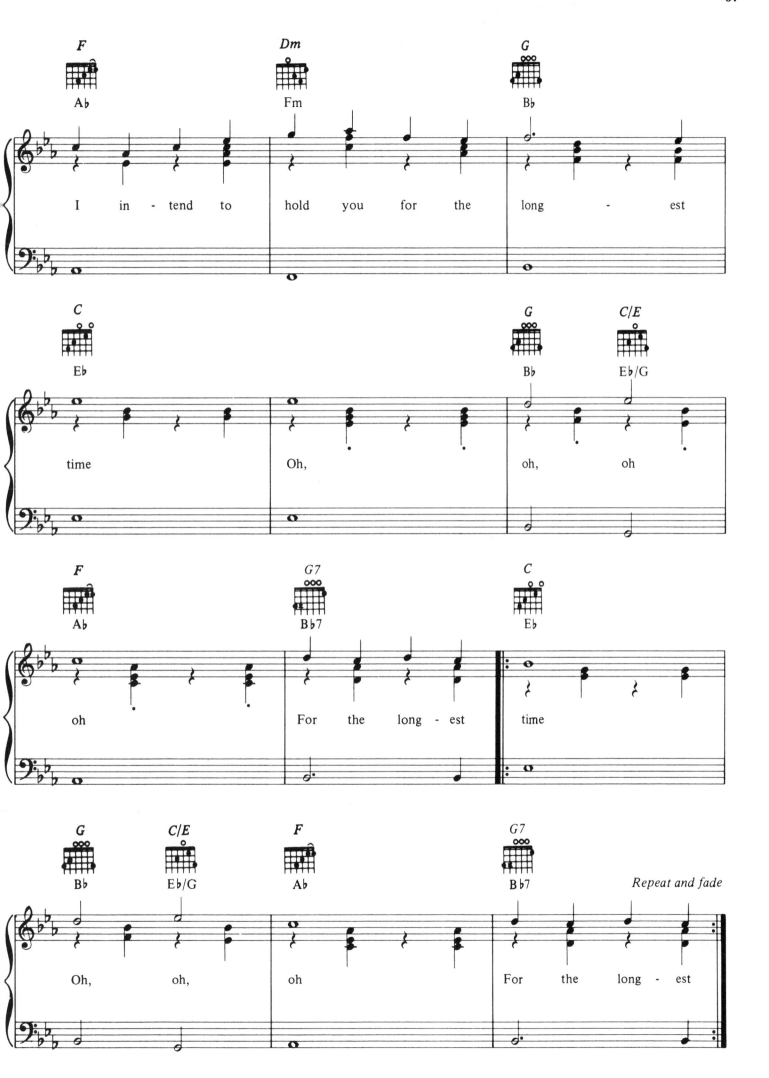

NEW YORK STATE OF MIND

Words and Music by
BILLY JOEL

the Dai - ly News

D.S. *for verse 3 & 5*

Coda

mind

ROSALINDA'S EYES

Words and Music by
BILLY JOEL

1. I play nights in the Span-
2. When she smiles,___ she gives ev-
3. All a - lone___ in a Puer-

ish part ___ of town. _____ I've got
'ry -thing___ to me. _____ When she's all___
to Ric - can band. _____ Un - ion wa-

SHAMELESS

Slow Rock beat

Words and Music by
BILLY JOEL

SHE'S GOT A WAY

Words and Music by
BILLY JOEL

STREETLIFE SERENADER

Words and Music by
BILLY JOEL

Street-life ser - e - nad - ers _____ have no ob - li -

ni - zing.